A FOOL OF GOD: THE MYSTICAL VERSE OF BABA TAHIR

A FOOL OF GOD: THE MYSTICAL VERSE OF BABA TAHIR

THE PERSIAN TEXT EDITED,
ANNOTATED AND TRANSLATED BY

EDWARD HERON-ALLEN

THE OCTAGON PRESS
LONDON

ISBN 900860 70 7

**Published for the Sufi Trust by
The Octagon Press**

First Published 1980
Reprinted 1987

Printed and bound in Great Britain at
The Camelot Press Ltd, Southampton

PREFACE

It has been seen that anything in the nature of a codex, or early and authoritative text of the Quatrains of Bābā Ṭāhir is yet to be found, but I have noted such as are worthy of remark in the Introduction to this volume.

For this version of the Quatrains of Bābā Ṭāhir, I have drawn from the following materials:

(i.) The well-known Bombay lithograph, containing the Rubā'iyāt of 'Omar Khayyām, Bābā Ṭāhir, Abu Sa'īd ibn Abu 'l-Khayr, &c. [Referred to as B or B i., and B ii.] رباعیات عمر خیام بابا طاهر ابو سعید بن ابو الخیر Bombay, 1297 A.H., and (second edition) Bombay, 1308 A.H. Both of these contain 57 rubā'iyāt. It was this collection which first called my attention to the author.

(ii.) The *Ātash Kadah* of Luṭf 'Alī Beg Āzar. [Referred to as AK.] Bombay, 1277 A.H. آتش کده لطف علی بیک آذر This contains 25 rubā'iyāt at p. 247.

(iii.) The *Majma'u 'l-Fuṣaḥā* of Riżā-Qulī Khān. [Referred to as M.] Ṭihrān, 1295 A.H. تذکرهٔ موسوم بمجمع الفصحا This contains 10 rubā'iyāt at p. 326 of vol. i.

(iv.) The collection lithographed at Ṭihrān (1274 A.H.), containing Rubā'iyāt of 'Omar Khayyām, Bābā Ṭāhir (27 rubā'iyāt), 'Aṭṭār, Malik Irij, and poems of Tabrīzī, &c. [Referred to as T.]

(v.) The *Munājāt* of the Khwāja 'Abdu 'llah al-Anṣārī. [Referred to as MA.] Bombay, 1301 A.H. مناجات خواجه عبد الله الانصارى This contains 32 rubā'iyāt at p. 87.

(vi.) The text constructed by M. Clément Huart in the Journal Asiatique (8th ser., vol. vi., no. 3, Paris, 1885, p. 502), purporting to be derived from nos. (i.), (ii.), and (iii.), and a modern MS. belonging to a contemporary collector, Mīrzā Ḥabīb Iṣfahānī, which I understand is now in Constantinople. [Referred to as H.]

(vii.) A MS. in my collection, which is undated, but appears to be of the end of the 18th or beginning of the 19th century, which contains 27 rubā'iyāt, three of which are not in any of the above sources. [Referred to as MS.]

رباعيات بابا طاهر همداني عريان

1.

خرم آنان که هر زامان ته وينن

سخون وا ته کرن وا ته نشينن

گرم پايی نه بی کآيم ته وينم

بشم آنون بوينم که ته وينن

B 5, AK 5, H 24, MS 5.

1. 1. Persian, هر زمان ترا بينند. The other texts for زامان read وامان, which is unsatisfactory.

1. 2. Persian, با تو نشينند. The other texts begin with the more ordinary form سخن. MS begins the line ته رازی کرن 'who confide their secrets to thee.'

1. 3. بود = بی ; ترا بينم = ته وينم ; اگر مرا = گرم. For B has دست نبی, AK has دسته نبی, and MS. has دست رس نبی پای نه بی, all of which convey a similar meaning.

1. 4. Persian, بشوم آنان ببينم که ترا بينند. The other texts restore the Persian آنان.

2.

بیته یا رب ببستان گل مرویاد

اگر رویاد هرگز کس مبویاد

بیته گر دل بخنده لب کشایه

رخش از خون دل هرگز مشویاد

B 49, T 4, H 2.

The dialectal forms to note in this quatrain are in
ll. 1 and 3, بیته for بی تو, and in l. 3 کشایه for کشاید.
B has the ordinary Persian form.

3.

خوشا آنان که الله یار شون بی

بحمد وقل هو الله کار شون بی

خوشا آنان که دائم در نمازن

بهشت جاودان بازار شون بی

B 26, T 12, H 46.

The terminals شون بی = شان بود.   T and B restore
شان.

l. 3.   T and B restore the Persian در نمازند.

4.

مو از قالوا بلی تشویش دیرم

گناه از برگ دارون بیش دیرم

چو فردا نومه خونون نومه خونن

مو در کف نومه سر در پیش دیرم

B 25, H 13.

The terminal دیرم in 1, 2 and 4 = دارم.

1. 1. مو = من. The line translates 'I am troubled on account of (the phrase) "They said Yes; (Thou art our Lord.)"'

1. 2. H has a somewhat pedantic note deriving دارون from دار ('a gallows') with a dialectal plural. It seems unnecessary to seek beyond دارَون = the common elm-tree, though B reads داران.

1. 3. In Persian, چون فردا نامه خوانان نامه خوانند, lit. 'When to-morrow the Readers of the book (i.e. the Recording Angels) read the Book.' B reads خونان and خونند.

1. 4. The same dialectal forms for من ـ نامه ـ دارم. B reads نامه.

5.

خداوندا که بوشم با که بوشم

مژه پر اشک خونین تا که بوشم

همم کز در برانی سو ته آیم

تو کم از در برانی واکه بوشم

B 30, H 16.

It will be observed that this quatrain is identical in sentiment, and almost textually as regards ll. 3 and 4, with B 2, AK 2, H 20, MS 2 (*infrâ*, No. 6).

The terminals بوشم are the dialectal form of باشم.

1. 1.   B has یا for با, and in l. 2 وا for تا, giving the interjectional ' Oh ! ' and ' Alas ! ' for the more satisfactory ' with ' and ' how long.'   It is probably a liberty or carelessness of the scribe.

1. 3.   I have followed H in taking سو تە as two words for سوی تو (' towards thee ') rather than as one for سوختە (' burnt,' or ' in ecstasy ').   برانند = برانن.   B restores the Persian form.

1. 4.   با = وا ; كە مرا = كم .   B has سو (' towards ') for وا or با.

6.

باین بی آشیانی بر کیانشم

باین بی خانمانی بر کیانشم

هم از در برانن سو تە آیم

تە گرا: د. برانی بر کیانشم

B 2, AK 2, H 20, MS 2.

Vide note to No. 5 *suprâ*.

l. 1.   کیانشم is the dialectal contraction of کیان (pl. of که) and شوم.

l. 2.   B and AK give the more ordinary Persian phrase خان و مانی.

l. 3.   The other texts give همم as in No. 5 *suprâ*.

l. 4.   The other texts, as in No. 5, give کم (= مرا که) for گر, a preferable variant.

7.

کشیمون ار بزاری از که ترسی
برانی ار بخواری از که ترسی
مو وا این نیمه دل ازکس نترسم
دو عالم دل ته داری از که ترسی

B 19, AK 20, H 41, T 26, M 10, MS 20.

l. 1.   The other texts begin the line کشیمان, M and MS substituting گر for ار; it is the dialectal form for اگر مارا کشی.

l. 2.   M and T have گر for ار; B, AK and MS have ور for ار. B has بخوانی for بخواری ('with contempt').

l. 3.   ما با = مو وا; the other texts, excepting M, have the مو at the end before نترسم, and begin با این.

l. 4.   ته = تو; M for دو عالم reads جهانی (syn.).

8.

اگر مستان مستیم از ته ایمون

و گر بی پا ودستیم از ته ایمون

اگر گوریم و ترسا و مسلمون

بهر ملّت که هستیم از ته ایمون

B 4, AK 4, MS 4, T 15, H 23.

The other texts restore the Persian ایمان all through (*vide* note on p. 69), and in the first two lines have the singular مستم - دستم.

l. 1.   B and the others have تو for ته here and in l. 2.

l. 3.   B and AK have گبر ('Guebres') for گور, and ور ('and if') for و.   AK and MS has هند ('Hindu') for ترسا; T reads the line اگر هند و اگر گبر ار مسلمان.   Every scribe seems to have chosen his own forms of unorthodoxy for insertion.

l. 4.   B and T تو for ته.

9.

نوای ناله غم اندوته ذونو

عیار زر خالص پوته ذونو

بوره سوته دلون واهم بنالیم

که حال سوته دل داسوته ذونو

B 56, AK 6, T 16, H 27.

The terminals نونو = the Persian داند ; MS has زونو
throughout, AK has it in ll. 2 and 4. Note the elimination of the خ in اندوته ـ پوته ـ سوته.

l. 1. This line in AK reads تو ای ناله و امد و ته زده نو.

l. 2. T has و قلت for زر, giving the meaning 'paucity
or pureness,' probably an error for قلب 'alloy'; MS has
و قلب in this place, giving 'alloyed or pure.' It might be
taken as an emphatic of خالص, but this would be far-fetched.

l. 3. دلان = دلون ; بیآ = بوره. T restores the Persian
forms ; MS and AK restore دلان only.

l. 4. The other texts for حال read قدر : 'The value (or
measure) of their initiation only the Initiates know.'

10.

هر اون باغی که دارش سر بدر بی
مدامش باغبان خونین جگر بی
بباید کندنش از بیخ و از بن
اگر بارش همه لعل و گهر بی

B 23, AK 24, T 27, H 45, MS 24.

Excepting for آن in l. 1 all the texts are unanimous as to
this quatrain, the intention of which completely baffles me.

11.

دلا راه ته پر خار و خسك بی

گذرگاه ته بر اوج فلك بی

گر از دستت بر آیو پوست از تن

بر افكن تا که بارت كمترك بی

B 20, AK 21, H 42, MS 21.

The meaning of this quatrain is exceedingly obscure.
بی = بود as before

1. 1.   B and AK restore the Persian تو; B has بر ('upon')
for پر (' full of ').

1. 2.   B and MS have تو.

1. 3.   MS reads در آیی for بر آیو; B and AK omit از
and begin اگر, and restore the Persian آید.   I think there
is a lost idiom here.

1. 4.   Note the diminutive comparative كمترك ' a little
less.'

12.

بوره سوته دلون گرد هم آییم

سخن وا هم کریم غمها کشاییم

ترازو آوریم غمها بسنجیم

هر آن سوته‌تریم سنگین‌تر آییم

B 46, H 19.

l. 1.   B has the Persian بیا and دلان.   سوته = سوخته.

l. 2.   B for واهم has باهم, giving us 'let us talk together' B also has کساریم ('let us suffer or undergo') for کشاییم, but the rhyme is impossible.   کنیم = کریم.

13.

بوره سوته دلون هون تا بناليم

زهجر آن گل رعنا بناليم

بشيم با بلبل شيدا بگلشن

اگر بلبل نناله ما بناليم

B 3, ak 3, ms 3, h 15.

l. 1.   In Persian, بیا سوخته دلان هان تا بنالیم.   All the other texts read سوته دلهای بوره تا بنالیم.   M. Huart has confused ll. 1 and 2 in his note, with a result which is, as he says, " unsatisfactory."

l. 2.   The other texts give عشق ('love') for هجر ('departure.')

l. 3.   بشویم = بشیم.

l. 4.   ننالد = نناله.   The other texts restore the Persian form.

14.

جرہ بازی بدم رفتم بہ نخچیر

سیہ چشمی بزد بربال مو تیر

برو غافل مچر در کوہساروں

ہر اوں غافل چرہ غافل خورہ تیر

B 35, H 5.

l. 2. B has دستی for چشمی, giving the meaning 'covetous' rather than 'ill-omened' or 'black-eyed,' and also من the Persian for the dialectal مو (= ما).

l. 3. Note the dialectal و, for ا in کوهساروں. B substitutes the word جوکناراں, giving us 'river-bank' instead of 'mountain-top.' The 1308 edition of B (but not the 1297 edition) مجو 'seek' for مچر 'graze' or 'wander.'

l. 4. Dialectal forms خورہ for چرہ ; چرہ for چرد ; اوں for آن ; for خورد. B restores the Persian form in each instance.

15.

دی اسب مرا گفت کہ در این چہ شکست

کاصطبل تو از زاویهای فلك است

نہ اب درآن نہ سبزہ نہ کاہ و جو

این جای ستور نیست جی ملك است

MS 27.

This quatrain, which is in pure Persian, is only to be found in the MS. no. vii. It is more than probably an interpolation (*vide* note on p. 72), and the metre is far from satisfactory.

16.

ز شور انگیزیٔ چرخ فلك بی

كه دائم چشم زخمم پر نمك بی

دمادم دود آهم تا سموات

تنم نالان و اشكم تا سمك بی

B 38, H 49.

l. 4. سمك is the mythological Fish that supports the whole world in the Muḥammadan cosmogony.

17.

خداوندا ز بس زارم ازین دل

شو و روزان در آزارم ازین دل

ز بس نالیدم از نالیدنم كس

ز مو بستون كه بیزارم ازین دل

B 29, H 9.

l. 2. The lithographer of B has the slip درازآرم, which is confusing for a moment.

l. 3. Mr. Browne suggests كشی for كس ' I have grieved so much : kill me with grief.'

l. 4. مو = ما ; بستون is the dialectal imperative of ستدن, and B reads بستان

18.

مو که سر در بیابونوم شو و روز

سرشک از دیده بارانوم شو و روز

نه تو دیرم نه جایوم میکرو درد

همی ذونم که نالونوم شو و روز

B 43, H 7.

Note the recurring dialectal form شو for شب (and in l. 3. تو for تب), and the pleonastic و in بیابونوم ‐ بارانوم ‐ جایوم ‐ نالونوم, all of which appear in restored Persian form in B, sc. بیابانم ‐ بارانم ‐ جایم ‐ نالانم.

l. 1. Dialectal form مو for من.

l. 3. تب for تو ‐ میکنم for میکرو ‐ دارم for دیرم.

l. 4. دانم for ذونم ; B has the Persian form.

19.

بلایه دل بلایه دل بلایه

گنه چشمون کرون دل مبتلایه

اگر چشمون نوینن روی زیبا

چه ذونو دل که خوبون درکجایه

B 17, AK 18, H 37, T 25, MS 18.

In all the other texts the final ه ه are omitted. They give here the value of است.

l. 1. T and MS substitute خدایا for the second بلای.

l. 2. Pers. چشمان, which is restored by the other texts. For کرون T has کرد, whilst the other texts have the participle کرن; کند would be a better emendation.

l. 3. چزمان; ندیدی = نوینی, but B and AK read نبینند, and زینا in AK are errors of the scribe. T and MS read the line اگر چشمان نکردی دیده بانی, 'If the eyes did not play the sentinel.'

l. 4. For نونو (in B and AK زونی) to balance (بلای) read Pers. خوبان = خوبین; داند. T and MS read the line چه دانستی دلم خوبان کجائی, 'How wouldst thou know, my heart, where the Beautiful Ones are?'

20.

ز دست دیده و دل هر دو فریاد

که هر چه دیده وینه دل کنه یاد

بسازم خنجری نیشش زپولاد

زنم بر دیده تا دل گده آزاد

B 36, H 3.

B has the ordinary Persian د instead of ذ at the end of each line.

l. 2.   Note the dialectal forms وینه for بیند, and کنه for کنذ. B restores the Persian forms.

l. 3.   بسازم is Persian, where one would have expected the dialectal form بسوجم. B for پولاذ has فولاذ, which is synonymous.

l. 4.   B has کردذ, for the dialectal form گرده.

21.

دلی دیره که بهبودش نمییبو

نصیحت می کرم سودش نمییبو

بباذش میدهم نش مییبرد باذ

برآتش می نهم دودش نمییبو

B 6, AK 7, H 26, T 17, M 2.

In the other texts the undotted د invariably takes the place of the ذ; نمییبو = نمییبوذ.

l. 1.   The other texts (except M) restore the Persian دارم.

l. 3.   M has مییبره for مییبرد, AK has بیادش and یاد, evidently an error of the scribe. نش compounded of نه and اش = اورا نه.

l. 4.   M has آذر for آتش, a synonym.

22.

مو آن رندم که نامم بی قلندر

نه خون دیرم نه مون دیرم نه لنگر

چو روز آیه بگردم کرد گیتی

چو شو گرده بخشتی وانهم سر

B 44, H 6.

l. 1.   Dialectal مو for من ـ بی for بود.

l. 2.   مان ـ خان for مون ـ خون 'possessions' or 'domestic belongings.' B has the variant line نه خون دیرم ز مون دیرم نه لنگر; دارم is the dialectal form of دیرم.

l. 3.   آیه for آید.

l. 4.   شو is dialectal for شب. B restores the Persian گردد for گرده.

23.

بعالم همچو مو پروانۀ نه

جهانرا همچو مو دیوانۀ نه

همه مارون و مورون لانه دیرن

من بیچاره را ویرانۀ نه

B 8, AK 9, H 28, T 18, MS 9.

The terminals نه stand for the Persian مو ; نیست in ll. 1 and 2 = مه.

l. 1.   The other texts read this line چو من یکسوته دل پروانهٔ نه. The word پروانه is especially applied to the moths that fly about a candle.   We have here a reference to the Sufi parable, in which the total annihilation of a moth by being burnt in a candle typifies the self-annihilation of the Initiate and his absorption into God.   The line as it reads in the other texts carries out the idea even more fully.

l. 2.   The other texts begin بعالم همچو مو, &c.

l. 3.   The other texts restore the Persian موران and ماران, and MS restores دارند for the dialectal دیرن.

l. 4.   The other texts for بیچاره return to the دیوانه of l. 2.

24.

ز کشت خاطرم جز غم نرویو

ز باغم بجز گل ماتم نرویو

ز صحرای دل بیحاصل مو

گیاه نا امیدی هم نرویو

B 47, T 1, H 35.

The terminals are the Persian نروید.   B and T have نروئی throughout.

l. 2.   For جز, B has جز, which gives correct scansion.

l. 3.   The other texts restore the Persian من for مو.

4.   The other texts eliminate the dot of ذ in امیدی.

25.

دلی نازك بسان شیشه ام بی

اگر آهی كشم اندیشه ام بی

سرشكم گر بوه خونین عجب نیست

مو آن دیرم كه ده خون ریشه ام بی

M 8, H 55.

l. 3.   نیست = بوه. M for بود has the dialectal form نی.

l. 4.   مو = من. M restores the Persian دارم.

26.

اگر دردم یكی بودی چه بودی

وگر غم اندكی بودی چه بودی

ببالینم حبیبم یا طبیبم

ازین دو گر یكی بودی چه بودی

B 42, H 52.

The texts are identical and pure Persian.

27.

بنالیدن دلم مانند نی بی

مدامم درد هجرانت زیی بی

مرا سوز و گدازه تا قیامت

خدا ذونو قیامترا که کی بی

B 21, AK 22, H 43, M 6, MS 22.

l. 1.   B and AK begin the line بند بند دلم, and MS بود; یی as before (= شوم) بند بند شم.

l. 3.   B, AK and MS read گدازت.

l. 4.   M has دانه (= داند) for ذونو; B, AK and MS read the line تا قیامت تا بکی بی خدا ز و, AK having تو for تا.

28.

بهار آیو بهر باغی گلی بی

بهر شاخی هزاران بلبلی بی

بهر مرزی نیارم پا نهادن

مباد از مو بترسوته دلی بی

B 50, T 6, H 54.

l. 1.   آید = آیو.   B and T have آئی.   B reads the line بهار آئی بهر لاله دلی بی.

l. 2.   The other texts begin بهر لاله.

l. 4.   سوخته = سوته; من = مو.

29.

مو آن بحرم که در ظرف آمدستم

مو آن نقطه که در حرف امدستم

بهرالفی الف قدّی بر آیه

الف قدّم که د. الف آمدستم

B 24, AK 25, H 22.

l. 1.   B and AK have من for مو here and in l. 2.

l. 3.   B and AK have برآید for برآیه the dialectal form.

30.

مو أم آن آفرین مرغی که در حال

بسوجم عالم ار برهم زنم بال

مصور گر کشه نقشم بدیوا،

بسوجم خونه از تاثیر تمثال

B 52, T 10, H 11.

l. 1.   مو = من.   Huart says that آفرین is an emendation suggested by Mīrzā Ḥabīb Iṣfahānī, whose MS. had the word عاجزین 'impotent' or 'hopeless,' which makes nonsense in this place.   B and T have identically منم for مو أم, فی العال ('in a moment') for در حال, and آجزین for آفرین.

l. 2.   بسوزم = بسوجم.   T omits هم, which is unimportant for the sense but not for the metre.

l. 3. كشه = كشد, and B and T have the latter (Persian) form.

l. 4. Persian, بسوزم خانه. B and T read عالم (' the universe') for خانه. B has تائيږ for تائير in *both* editions, which would seem to preclude a mistake of the copyist, but is incomprehensible.

31.

اكر دل دلبره دلبر چه نومه

وكر دلبر دله دل از چه نومه

دل و دلبر بهم آميته ديرم

نذونم دل كهه دلبر كرومه

B 13, AK 14, MS 14, T 21, H 32.

l. 1. نومه (here and in l. 2) = نام است. T reads this line اكر دل دلبر و دلبر كدامست, the other texts ending the line كدامى.

l. 2. وكر دلبر دل و دلبرا چه = دل است. T reads دله, نامست, the other texts having دل از for دلرا and ending چه نامى; they also have دلى for دله, as is frequent.

l. 3. اميته = آميخته. The other texts for ديرم have ينم = بينم.

l. 4. نذونم = ندانم; كهه = كه است; كرومه = كدامست or كدامى, which forms are retained by T, B, AK and MS.

T has و که for کهه ; B, AK and MS begin the line نـزونم .
AK has خبر که 'what news' for کهه .

The meaning of the whole quatrain is very mystic and
purposely involved.

32.

بروی دلبری کر مائلستم

مکن منعم گرفتار دلستم

خدارا ساربون آهسته میرون

که مو واماندهٔ آن قافله ستم

B 51, T 9, H 21.

The terminations ستم represent the auxiliary هستم .

l. 2.   The م in منعم is the accusative after مکن .

l. 3.   B and T restore the Persian forms ساربان and
میران .

l. 4.   B restores من for مو , and has قافلستم for قافله ستم .

The imagery in this quatrain is obscure, but I take it
to mean, 'I lag behind in the race for life, making love,
and meanwhile life passes.'   Cf. Omar Khayyām, قافله عمر
'the Caravan of Life';   and also Mr. E. G. Browne's
quotation from Quṭbu 'd-Dīn 'Atīqī, at p. 51 of his recent
'Biographies of Persian Poets' (Journ. Roy. Asiatic Soc.,
Jan. 1901): 'Every moment I fall back from this caravan;

again and again I turn my face towards the abode of that swaying cypress.'

33.

ز دل نقش جمالت در نشی یا

خیال خط و خالت در نشی یا،

مژه سازم بگرد دیده پرچین

که خون ریژه خیالت در نشی یا.

н 4, м 1.

ll. 1, 2 and 4.   Note the dialectal form نشی for نشود.

l. 3.   M has کردم for سازم, which is synonymous.

l. 4.   ریژه is the dialectal form of ریزد.   M begins the line که خونایه, a dialectal form of the equivalent خون آید.

34.

کارم همه ناله و خروش است امشب

نه صبر پدید است و نه هوش است امشب

دوشم خوش بود ساعتی پنداری

کفّارهٔ خوش دلئ دوش است امشب

мs 26.

This quatrain is in pure Persian, and only found in the MS. no. vii.

35.

هزارت دل بغارت برده ویشه

هزارانت جگر خون کرده ویشه

هزاران داغ ویش از رویشم اشمرت

هنی نشمرته از اشمرته ویشه

B 11, AK 12, M 5, T 20, H 39, MS 12.

The terminals ویشه = بیش است. The terminals of M and T are ویش, and of B, AK and MS بیشی.

1. 1.   M and T for بردُ have the dialectal برتهُ; B and AK have ورته; MS between this and T has ورته و بیشی. M. Huart has misread the termination in AK, which is very badly written.

1. 2.   The same observations apply here.

1. 3.   In T the final ت is omitted. The various scribes have taken considerable liberties with this line, probably not understanding it; thus M has سنیم for ویشم, B and AK have ریش ازسیم for ویش از ویشم.

1. 4.   M for هنی (dialectal form of هنوز) has the prefix همی. The form اشمرته, which is to be found also in M, T, B and AK, does not rhyme. MS is the only text before me which has اشمرده, which would rhyme correctly in this quatrain as it stands here.

36.

پریشان سنبلان پر تاو مکّه
خماربن نرگسان خوناو مکّه
وریڼی تہ کہ مهر از ما وریڼی
وریڼہ روزگار اشتاو مکّه

B 7, AK 8, H 31, MS 8.

مکّه is the dialectal imperative of کردن.

l. 1.　The other texts read تاب for تاو.

l. 2.　The others for خوناو read پر خواب 'full of sleep.' نرگیسان in H is a misprint.

l. 3.　وریڼی = بریڼی, which is the dialectal form of وریڼی 'thou art bent on,' in distinction from بر این هستی at the end of the line, which is derivable from بریدن 'to sever.' MS for تہ has خود ('self').

l. 4.　اشتاو = اشتاب ; بریڼہ = بریند.

37.

دلت ای سنگدل برما نسوجہ
عجب نبوہ اگر خارا نسوجہ
بسوجم تا بسوجونم دلت را
در آتش چوب تر تنها نسوجہ

B 33, T 7, H 34.

The terminals نسوزد = نسوجه. The terminals in T read
نسوجی, and in B نسوتی (from سوختن).

l. 2.   نبود = نبوه. The Persian form is restored in B,
which ends بسوتی.

l. 3.   بسوزانم = بسوجونم ; بسوزم = بسوجم. B and T have
the compromise بسوجانم.

l. 4.   For آتش B has آزر, and T has آذر.

38.

دلی دیرم ز عشقت گیژ وویژه
مژه بر هم زنم سیلابه خیژه
دل عاشق مثال چوپ تربی
سری سوژه سری خونابه ریژه

B 15, AK 16, T 23, MS 16, H 29.

AK and MS end l. 1 رویجی, l. 2 خیجی, l. 4 ریجی.
The whole quatrain with its variations gives us a good idea
of the elasticity of the dialect in which it is written.

l. 1.   ببیزد = وویژه ; دارم = دیرم. T reads the line
دلم از دست خوبان گیم ریجه (ریزد = ریجه), the poet's heart
being broken by the power of Beauties in general. B, AK
and MS are the same, but soften دست into عشق.

l. 2.   T reads this line گهی سوجه بر آتش که بریجه 'At one
time burns upon the fire, at another crumbles away.' (سوجه
= سوزد ; بریجه = بریزد).

l. 3. بی = بود . B, AK and MS have بسان for مثال, a synonym.

l. 4. T has سوجه and ریجه, and the 1297 edition of B has سوجی (like AK), a phonetic error of the scribe. سوجه and سوجی = سوزد from سوختن.

B 45 is a slightly variant repetition of this quatrain :—

دلی دیرم رعشقت گیژ ویژه
مژه بر هم زنم خونابه ریژه . &c.

39.

بی ته یکدم دلم خرّم نمونه
وگر روی تو وینم غم نمونه
اگر درد دلم قسمت نموین
دل بی درد در عالم نمونه

B 18, AK 19, MS 19, H 36.

The terminals نمونه = the Persian نماند ; the other terminate in نمانی. The occurrence in the qua' both forms ته and تو is noteworthy.

l. 2. بینم = وینم.

l. 3. نموین is the dialectal form of یایند restored by the other texts.

40.

مسلسل زلف بر رو ریته دیری

گل و سنبل بهم آمیته دیری

پریشان چون کری اون تار زلفون

بهر تاری دلی آویته دیری

B 22, AK 23, H 44, MS 23.

The terminals دیری = داری. Note also the dialectal forms of ریخته ـ آمیخته ـ آویخته.

1. 3. B and AK have زآن for چون, and restore (also MS) اون for آن.

41.

خور آفین چهره‌ات افروته‌تر بی

دلم از تیر عشقت دوته‌تر بی

ز چه خال رخت ذونی سیاهه

هرآن نزدیک خور بی سوته‌تر بی

M 7, H 57.

In this quatrain we have the dialectal forms of افروخته ـ سوخته ـ دوخته.

1. 3. دانی = ذونی. The terminal ه = است. M restores دانی, and has سیاهن the plural form.

42.

نسیمی کز بن آن کاکل آیو

مرا خوشتر زبوی سنبل آیو

بشو گیرم خیالش را در آغوش

سحر از بسترم بوی گل آیو

B 14, ak 15, h 25, m 3, t 22, ms.

The terminals آیو = آید, which is restored in M and AK. B, T and MS have آیی all through.

1. 1.   MS for کز بن آن reads کز درون, giving the sense from among those curls.'

1. 3.   M, B, AK, T and MS begin the line چو شو.   H notes هرشو from the Isfahānī MS. شو is the dialectal form of شب.   The other texts read خیالترا.

43.

دو زلفونت کشم تار ربابم

چه می خواهی ازین حال خرابم

تو که بمو سر یاری نداری

چرا هر نیمه شو آیی بخوابم

B 41, h 18, t 5.

l. 1. B and T preserve the Persian زلفانت. B has بسو for کشم, which is unsatisfactory. The Rebāb is a two- or three-stringed bow instrument, played like a violoncello, much in use in Persia, which I have described elsewhere ('Violin Making,' London, 1885, p. 27).

l. 3. T has با ما for بمو, تو که بمو for اگر با من, and B has correcting the metre, which is wrong, as above. Mr. Browne suggests تو گر با مو. These are clearly allowable emendations.

l. 4. نیمه شو (Pers. شب), ' midnight.'

44.

ته کت نازنده چشمون سرمه سایه

ته کت بالنده بالا دلربایه

ته کت مشکینه گیسو در قفایه

ابی واجی که سر گردون چرایه

B 10, AK 11, H 38, MS 11.

In ll. 1, 2 and 3 تو که ترا = ته کت. The other texts omit the final ه.

l. 1. The other texts restore the Persian چشمان. I am not quite satisfied whether سرمه سایه should be rendered ' shadowed with surmeh,' or ' are rubbed with surmeh,' giving to the terminal ه the power of است. B has the reading سائی, the 2nd person singular, which is probably the proper reading.

l. 2.   In this line the terminal ه = است.

l. 3.   تفائی in B 1297 and نقائی in B 1308 are errors of the scribes.

l. 4.   M. Huart appends the following note :—" This line is nearly incomprehensible. واجی must approximate the Talish واج ('word,' Bérésine, p. 52) .... بد واجی signifies 'evil word' (Bérésine, p. 30) ... But چرایه seems to be a 3rd pers. sing. of the aorist; we connect it with چریدن 'to wander,' which we have already met bearing this meaning. *Cet hémistiche est rebelle a l'analyse et notre traduction très conjecturale.*" I would rather cling to the primary meaning of چرا, and suggest as a translation, 'O Refuser of Speech, wherefore is thy head averted?' Mr. Browne suggests the rendering, 'Why dost thou ask "Wherefore art thou dizzy?"' making چرایه = چرائی .

45.

چو خوش بی مهربانی هر دو سربی
که یك سر مهربانی درد سربی
اگر مجنون دل شوریدهٔ داشت
دل لیلی ازآن شوریدهتر بی

B 9, ᴀᴋ 10, ᴛ 19, ʜ 48, ᴍꜱ 10.

All the texts are identical and, save for the contracted dialectal terminal بی, are in pure Persian.

l. 1.   Compare the Turkish proverb محبّت ایکی باشدندر 'Love must be on both sides.' Mr. Browne tells me that in Persia the word از is substituted for هر.   It is certainly better. B ii. begins the line چه for چو.

ll. 3 and 4.   Leila and Majnūn represent in Persian poetry the archetype of profoundest love.

46.

بوره یکشو منوّر کن وثاقم

مهل در محنت روز فراقم

بجفت طاق ابروی تو سوگند

که مو جفت غمم از تو طاقم

B 37, H 12.

The variations between H and B are very considerable in this verse, B as a rule substituting the Persian for the dialectal forms.

l. 1.   بوره = بیا ; شو = شب. آمدن; the imperative of آمدن. B's line reads—

بیا یکشو برافروزون اطاقم

l. 2.   مهل neg. imp. of هشتن or هلیدن.   B's line reads

محل در محنت و درد و فراقم

l. 3.   B's line merely transposes thus:—بطاق جفت.

Note the word-play upon جفت and طاق ; طاق also meaning 'single' as opposed to جفت 'a pair.'

l. 4.   تب = تو ; من = مو . B's line reads—

که هم جفت غمم تا از تو طاقم

retaining the Persian value of تو .

47.

مگر شیر و پلنگی ایدل ایدل

بمو دایم بجنگی ایدل ایدل

اگر دستم فتی خونت وریژم

ووبنم تاچه زنگی ایدل ایدل

B 1, H 8, AK 1, MS 1.

l. 2.   Dialectal form بمو for بما .

l. 3.   فتی is the dialectal form of the Persian افتادی ;
وریژم = Persian بریزم , MS has the form بریجم .

l. 4.   ووبنم is the Persian ببینم . B gives the compromise بوینم .

48.

نگارینا دل وجانم ته دیری

همه پیدا و نهانم ته دیری

نذونم مو که این درد از که دیرم

همی فونم که درمانم ته دیری

M 9, H 56.

In the terminals توداری = ته دیری.

l. 2. M for نهانم has the synonym پنهانم, which is required by the metre, which halts here.

l. 3. M for نذونم مو has the strong Persian form نمیدانم.

l. 4. دانم = ذونم.

49.

اگر آیی بجانت وا نوازم

وگر نآیی زهجرانت گدازم

هراون دردی که داری بر دلم نه

بمیرم یا بسوجم یا بسازم

B 34, T 2, H 17.

F. Rückert cites this verse with certain variants in his 'Grammatik und Rhetorik der Perser' (Gotha, 1874, p. 22); but he does not cite his authority, and the Grand-Ducal librarian at Gotha tells me there is no MS. or lithograph of Bābā Ṭāhir in the library there.

T and B restore the Persian ز for ذ all through.

l. 1. Rückert has نواجم.

l. 2. T and Rückert have بهجرانت, Rückert following grammatically with بساجم ('I will put up with it'), the dialectal form of بسازم.

l. 3.   B and Rückert have the Persian هرآن for هراون,
whilst T substitutes بيا 'come!'

l. 4.   The forms are much interchanged.   T has بسوزم.
B has بساجم (which does not rhyme); and so has Rückert,
who also has تا for the first يا, and translates 'sterben will
ich, mir mag weh oder wohl sein,' which, if supported by
authority, is good.   Cf. the philosophical axiom—

اگر قضا با تو نسازد ـ تو با قضا بساز

50.

الاله كوهسارون هفته بى
بنوشه جو كنارون هفته بى
منادى مى كرم شهرو بشهرو
وفاى گلعذارون هفته بى

B 16, AK 17, T 24, H 40, MS 17.

In ll. 1, 2, 4 we have the dialectal plural in ون instead
of ان; the other texts have the Persian بى = ان; بود.

l. 1.   هفته 'of one week's duration' (Pers. يك هفتگى).
Cf. يك سالگى 'one year old.'   The hamza in الاله in H
injures the metre.   So also بنوشه in l. 2.

l. 2.   T and MS restore the Persian form بنفشه.

l. 3.   B and AK have ميكرو for مى كرم; MS restores the
Persian شهران بشهران.   B has سهرو بسهرو probably an omission

of the scribe.   Connected with the Arabic سهر it might be read ' in every waking moment,' *sed quœre*.

l. 4.   ان = ون .

51.

دلم از درد تو دائم غمینه

ببالین خشتم و بستر زمینه

. همین جرمم که مو تە دوست دیرم

نه هرکت دوست دارە حالش اینه

B 53, M 4, H 30, T 11.

The terminals ه represent the Persian است .

l. 1.   تو is probably an emendation of the scribe. تە is in l. 3, and in T here also.   M for تو دائم has هجرانت ('thine absence').   از for H's ز; for metre.

l. 2.   M reads this line سر نیم خشت و بالینم زمینه , a paraphrase.

l. 3.   Compare دیرم in this line with the purer but still dialectal form دارە in l. 4.   M begins the line with the paraphrase گناهم اینکه مو &c.;   B restores the Persian دارم .   Cf. Othello, ' Think on thy sins.'   D. ' They are loves I bear to you.'

l. 4.   که ترا = کت .   M for هرکت has هرانکت , and T and B restore دارە to دارد .

52.

مو آن شمعم که اشکم آذرین بی

کسی کو سوته دل اشکش نه این بی

همه شو سوجم و گریم همه روز

ز ته شامم چنون روزم چنین بی

B 48, T 3, H 53.

l. 1.   مو = من ;   T and B for آذرین read از زمین, which is unsatisfactory. Cf. the rubāʻī of Ḥāfiz, beginning :—
در هجر تو من ز شمع افزون گریم ' When thou art absent I weep more than a taper.'

l. 2.   که اوسوخته = کو سوته ; T has که for کو, and both the other texts have چنین for نه این, robbing the line of its interrogative form.

l. 3.   شب سوزم = شو سوجم . The other texts restore شب.

l. 4.   The other texts have چنون for چنین .

53.

بیته اشکم زمژگان تر آیو

بیته نخل امیدم بی بر آیو

بیته در کنج تنهائی شو و روز

نشینم تا که عمرم بر سر آیو

B 32, T 8, H 33.

T and B end in آیی the other dialectal form of آید
بیتو = بیته.

l. 1.   B reads بموكان.

l. 2.   For امیدم T reads حیاتم ('my tree *of life*').

l. 3.   همه عمر T reads شب و روز .شب = شو. For 'all my life.'

l. 4.   For که عمرم T has the synonym حیاتم, as in l. 2.

54.

دلا پوشم ز هجرت جامهٔ نیل
كشم بار غمت چون جامه بر نیل
دم از مهرت زنم همچون دم صبح
ازین دم تا دم صور سرافیل

в 28, н 10.

This quatrain may have suffered severe emendation, but, as it is, it is free from dialectal forms. Note the pun on مهر ('love' and 'sun') in l. 3. Compare l. 1 with the lines introduced (from Farīdu 'd-Dīn 'Attār) by FitzGerald into his 'Omar Khayyām, 'The seas that mourn in flowing purple, of their Lord forlorn.'

55.

مدامم دل پر آذر دیده تر بی

خم عیشم پر از خون جگر بی

ببویت زندگی یابم پس از مرگ

ترا گر بر سر خاکم گذر بی

B 31, H 47.

The two texts are identical save for ازر (B) in l. 1.
Compare Omar Khayyām, who inverts this sentiment (Cal-
cutta MS. 16, FitzGerald's translation 92):

تا بر سر خاك من رسد مخموری

از بوی شراب من شود مست و خراب

56.

درد یست اجل که نیست درمان اورا

بر شاه و وزیر هست فرمان اورا

شاهی که بحکم دوش کرمان میخورد

امروز همین خورند کرمان اورا

MS 25.

It will be observed that this quatrain, which has a
ring of 'Omar Khayyām rather than of Bābā Ṭāhir, is

in pure Persian, and I have only found it in the MS. no. vii.

ll. 3 and 4. Note the play upon the word كرمان, which means in l. 3 the town of Kirmān, and in l. 4 is the plural of كرم 'a worm.' A precisely similar distich occurs in the first chapter of the Būstān of Saʿdī :

طمع كرده بودم كه كرمان خورم

كه ناگه بخوردند كرمان سرم

I had a desire to conquer Kirmān,
When suddenly *the worms* devour me.

And Firdawsī also makes use of the same word-play in his account of the Great Worm of Haftawād, from which, according to him, Kirmān derived its name.

57.

سیه بختم كه بختم سر نگون بی

توه روژم كه روژم واژگون بی

شدم خار و خس كوه محبّت

ز دست دل كه یا رب غرق خون بی

B 40, ʜ 51.

l. 2.   روز = روژ ; تباه = توه.   B for توه reads سیه as in l. 1.

58.

از آنروزی که مارا آفریدی

بغیر از معصیت از ما چه دیدی

خداوندا بحق هشت و چارت

ز مو بگذ، شتر دیدی نه دیدی

T 14, B 55, H 58.

l. 2.　T for از ما چه دیدی has چیزی ندیدی .

l. 3.　Literally, ' by the faith of thy Eight and Four,' *i.e.* the Twelve Imāms of the Faith.

l. 4.　T restores مه. The مو in this line is the only sign of the dialect, and is probably an emendation of the scribe.　The whole quatrain is probably spurious. M. Huart appends a note :—' A proverbial expression. Oriental wisdom teaches that it is sometimes dangerous to have seen an escaped camel '; and cites the apologue of Zadig and the horse of the King of Babylon.　He evidently was unacquainted with the Turkish proverb (which has equivalents all over Asia), اولوم قره دوه در که هر قپوده چوکر, ' Death is a black camel which kneels at everybody's door.' The quatrain is merely an address to God pleading for a longer life.

59.

غم دوران نصیب جان ما بی

ز درد ما فراغت کیمیا بی

رسه آخر بدرمون درد مر کس

دل ما بی که درمونش فنا بی

B 39, H 50.

Identical save that B restores رسد in l. 3, and درمان in ll. 3 and 4 ; بی as before.

60.

بشم واشم ازین عالم بدر شم

بشم از چین و ماچین دیرتر شم

بشم از حاجیان حج بپرسم

که این دیری بسه یا دیرتر شم

B 27, H 14.

The texts agree in this quatrain, and the only dialectal peculiarities are the elimination of the و in شَوَم all through, and the form بسه in l. 4, in which ه = است (Pers. بس است), and دور for دیر.

61.

نگار تازه خیز مو کجائی

بچشمون سرمه ریز مو کجائی

نفس بر سینهٔ طاهر رسیده

دم رفتن عزیزم مو کجائی

B 57, H 59.

B restores the Persian ما all through, and in l. 2 چشمان.
In l. 3 we find the common idiom for the point of death.
Cf. 'Omar Khayyām (Whinfield's text, no. 134) چون جان
بلب آمد, and Sa'di (Gulistān, chap. i. 16) بسی جان
بلب آمد, *et passim.*

62.

ته که نا خواندهٔ علم سموات

ته که نا بردهٔ پی در خرابات

ته که سود و زیان خود نذونی

بمردون کی رسی هیهات هیهات

B 54, T 13, H 1.

l. 2. T has ٤ر, for پی, giving the equivalent 'made thy
way' for 'set thy foot' (in the tavern).

l. 3. نذونی = the Persian ندانی, in which amended form we find it in B and T.

l. 4. بمردون = (Pers.) بمردان. B and T begin the line بیاران, giving us the more mystic ' friends (of God) ' for the vaguer ' mankind.'

The poet wishes to convey that if a man has neither the self-denial of asceticism nor the courage of his contrary convictions, he is not fit to be admitted among men of decided character.

THE

LAMENT OF BĀBĀ ṬĀHIR

PROSE TRANSLATION

PROSE TRANSLATION
OF THE FOREGOING TEXT.

———————◆•◉•◆———————

Note.—In the following translation I have endeavoured to offer a certain measure of ordinary English expression. Where the precisely literal signification has suffered eclipse, it has been restored in the notes. The notes appended to the foregoing text must also be referred to when characteristic Oriental images occur in this translation.

1.

Happy are they who live in the sight of Thee,[1]
Who hang upon Thy words,[2] and dwell with Thee,
Too frail to approach, I see Thee from afar,
And seek the sight of those that see Thee ever.[3]

2.

Without Thee in the Garden, Lord, may no rose bloom,
Or, blooming, may none taste its sweet perfume,
So, should my heart expand when Thou art not nigh,
'Twere vain! my heart's grief naught could turn to joy.[4]

---

[1] *Lit.* who see Thee always.   [2] *Lit.* who talk with Thee.

[3] *Lit.* Though I have not strength (a foot) to come and see Thee, I will go and see those who see Thee.

[4] *Lit.* If, without Thee, the heart smiles and opens its lips (in laughter), may it never wash its cheek from heart's blood.

3.

Happy are they indeed whose Friend is God,
Who, giving thanks, say ever, *"He is God!"*;[1]
Happy are they who always are at prayer,
Eternal Heaven is their just reward.[2]

4.

That phrase, *"They said 'Yes!'"* fills me with alarm,
I bear more sins than does a tree bear leaves;
When, on the last day, "They-that-read-the-Book"
    shall read,
I, bearing such a record, will hang my head.

5.

Lord! who am I, and of what company?
How long shall tears of blood thus blind mine eyes?
When other refuge fails I'll turn to Thee,
And if Thou failest me, whither shall I go?

---

[1] "Whose (constant) occupation is the reciting of the Ḥamd and the Ikhlāṣ," i.e. the Sūratu 'l-Fātiḥa, the first chapter of the Qur'ān, beginning الحمد لله "Thanks be to God," and the Sūratu 'l-Ikhlāṣ, the 112th chapter of the Qur'ān, beginning قل هو الله احد "Say: He is one God."

[2] *Lit.* Their market, i.e. the market in which their wares find acceptance.

6.

Homeless as I am, to whom shall I apply?
A houseless wanderer, whither shall I go?
Turned from all doors, I come at last to Thee,
If thy door is denied, where shall I turn?

7.

If Thou killest me miserably—whom fearest Thou?
And if Thou driv'st me forth abject—whom fearest
 Thou?
Though a half-hearted thing, *I* fear none,
Thy heart is the two worlds—whom fearest Thou?

8.

Drunkards and drunk though we be, Thou art our
 Faith,[1]
Unstable, weak though we be, Thou art our Faith,
Though we be Muslims, Guebres, Nazarenes,
Whate'er the Outward Form,[2] Thou art our Faith.

   *   *   *   *

---

[1] Perhaps we should read instead of ايمان "faith," امان
"quarter" or "mercy," in which case the lines would end, "(we
ask) quarter from Thee."
[2] *Lit.* In whatsoever faith (or sect) we be, &c.

9.

He who has suffered grief knows well its cry,
As knows the Assayer[1] when gold is pure ;
Come then ye Burnt-in-Heart, chaunt we laments,[2]
For well we know what 'tis to Burn-in-Heart.[3]

10.

When o'er the Garden wall the branches hang,
The garden's keeper suffers ever bitter grief,
They must be cut back, even to the roots,
Even though pearls and rubies be their fruit.

11.

Briar and thorn beset thy way, O Heart,
Beyond the Dome of Heaven is thy road ;[4]
If thou art able, then thy very skin
Cast off from thee, and lighten thus thy load.[5]

---

[1] *Lit.*   the Crucible.
[2] *Lit.*   let us lament together.
[3] *Lit.*   For he whose heart is burnt knows the condition of the Burnt-in-Heart.
[4] *Lit.*   Thy passage must be over the Zenith of Heaven.
[5] *Lit.*   If it comes from thy hand (i.e. if thou canst), cast off thy skin, so that thy load may thus be a little less.

12.

Come, O ye Burnt-in-Heart, let us gather round,
Let us converse, setting forth our woes,
Bring scales, make trial of our weight of woe,
The more we burn, the heavier weighs our grief.[1]

13.

O Burnt-in-Heart, come ye and mourn with me,
Mourn we the flight of that most lovely Rose ;
Hie we with the ecstatic Nightingale to the Rose-
    Garden,
And when she ceases mourning,[2] we will mourn.

14.

A falcon I ! and, as I chased my prey,
An evil-eyed-one's arrow[3] pierced my wing ;
Take heed ye Heedless ! wander not the heights,[4]
For, him who heedless roams,[5] Fate's arrow strikes.

*   *   *   *

---

[1] *Lit.* the heavier will we weigh (i.e. the greater will be our honour).

[2] *Lit.* And though she mourn not.

[3] This might also mean " A black-eyed beauty's arrow," which is probably correct.

[4] *Lit.* feed (pasture), not on the heights.

[5] *Lit.* feeds (grazes).

15.

My horse said yesterday to me: "There is no doubt
" But that your stable is a coign of Heaven ;
" Here is not grass nor water, straw nor grain,
" 'Tis fit for Angels, not for beasts like me!"[1]

* * * *

16.

'Tis Heaven's whim to vex me, and distress,[2]
My wounded eyes hold ever briny tears,
Each moment soars the smoke of my despair to heaven,
My tears and groans fill all the Universe.[3]

17.

O Lord ! this heart of mine afflicts me sore,[4]
I weep[5] this heart of mine both day and night ;
Often I grieve but for my grief ; O Some-one
Rid me of this heart that I may be free.[6]

---

[1] This is ascribed to Bābā Ṭāhir in my MS., but I think it is an importation.   It is neither in his style or language.

[2] *Lit.* 'Tis through the mischief-working of Heaven's Wheel that…

[3] *Lit.* My groaning body and my tears reach even unto Samak (i.e. the Fish that in the Muḥammadan cosmogony supports the whole world, here meant to symbolize the deepest depths of ocean).

[4] *Lit.* O Lord ! so afflicted am I by this heart.

[5] *Lit.* I am in torment through this heart of mine, &c.

[6] *Lit.* for I am weary of it. *Vide* also the note on p. 32.

18.

By day and night the desert is my home,
By day and night mine eyes shed bitter tears,
No fever rocks me, I am not in pain,
All I know is that day and night I grieve.

19.

O wicked, wanton, wastrel heart of man,[1]
When the eyes sin the heart must bear the doul[2]:
If the eyes never saw a lovely face,
How would the heart e'er know where beauties are ?

20.

Beneath the tyranny of eyes and heart I cry,
For, all that the eyes see, the heart stores up:
I'll fashion me a pointed sword of steel,
Put out mine eyes, and so set free my heart.

21.

Mine is a heart that has no health in it,
Howe'er I counsel it, it profits not ;
I fling it to the winds, the winds will none of it,
I cast it on the flames,—it does not burn.[3]

---

[1] *Lit.* A plague is the heart, a plague, a plague.
[2] *Or,* "The eyes see, and the heart is afflicted (with love).
[3] *Lit.* it does not smoke.

22.

I am that wastrel called a Kalandar,
I have no home, no country, and no lair,[1]
By day I wander aimless o'er the earth,
And when night falls, my pillow is a stone.

23.

What blundering Moth in all the World like me?
What madman like me in the Universe?
The very Serpents and the Ants have nests,
But I—poor wretch—no ruin shelters me.

24.

The Meadow of my Thought grows naught save grief,
My Garden bears no flower save that of woe;
So arid is the desert of my heart,
Not even the herbage of despair grows there.

25.

My heart is dainty as a drinking cup,
I fear for it whene'er I heave a sigh;
It is not strange my tears are as blood,
I am a tree whose roots are set in blood.

---

[1] *Lit.* anchor (i.e. settled abode).

26.

If single were my grief, what should I care ?[1]
If small my sorrow were, what should I care ?
Call to my couch my lover or my leech,
If either one were nigh what should I care ?

*   *   *   *

27.

With wailing plaint my heart is like a flute,
The grief of losing thee is ever at my heels ;
Till the Last Day am I consumed with grief,
And when that Day shall be, God only knows.

28.

'Tis Spring ! in every garden roses bloom,
On every bough a thousand nightingales ;
There is no mead where I can set my foot,
Pray there be none more Burnt-in-Heart than I.

*   *   *   *

---

[1] *Lit.* what (harm) would it be ?

29.

I am the ocean poured into a jug,[1]
I am the point essential to the letter;
In every thousand one greater man stands out,[2]
I am the greater man of this mine Age!

30.

A Phoenix I, whose attributes are such
That when I beat my wings, the World takes fire;
And should a Painter limn me on a wall,
Mine Image being there would burn the house.

*   *   *   *

31.

If my Sweetheart is my heart, how shall I name her?
And if my heart is my Sweetheart, whence is she named?
The two are so intimately interwoven that
I can no longer distinguish one from the other.

---

[1] I.e. an infinite soul in a finite body. Cf. the passage in the Prologue to Book I. of the Mathnawī of Jalālu 'd-dīn Rūmī: "If thou pourest the ocean into a jug, how much will go into it? But one day's portion "—

گر بریزی بحر را در کوزه

چند گنجد قسمت یك روزه

[2] *Lit.* in stature (upright) like an *Alif* (i.e. the Persian letter ا "a").

32.

If the mood takes me to seek my Loved One's face,
Restrain me not, my heart is thrall to her ;[1]
Ah, Camel-man, for God's sake haste not so !
For I am a laggard behind the Caravan.

*   *   *   *

33.

The picture of thy Beauty, Love, quits not my heart,
The down, the mole, Love, on thy cheek I see alway ;[2]
I'll knit my lashes close, o'er wrinkled eyes,
That, weeping, thine image ne'er can leave me, Love.[3]

34.

To-night I can do nought but weep and wail,
To-night I am impatient, conscienceless ;[4]
Last night one hour seemed passing sweet to me,
To-night 'twould seem, I pay for last night's joy.

---

[1] *Lit.* I am the thrall of my heart.
[2] *Lit.* The image of thy down, thy mole, Love, will not depart.
[3] *Lit.* That (though) blood (i.e. bitter tears) pour forth, thine image may not go forth.
[4] *Lit.* beside myself.

35.

More than a thousand hearts hast thou laid waste,
More than a thousand suffer grief for thee,
More than a thousand wounds of thine I've counted,
Yet the uncounted still are more than these.

36.

Subdue the glories of thine hyacinthine hair,
Wipe the tears of blood from thy narcissus-eyes ;
Why robb'st thou me of the Sun—which is thy love ?
Day passes quick, bring not the night too soon !¹

37.

O heart of Stone, thou burnest not for me,²
That stone burns not, is not, indeed, so strange ;
But I will burn till I inflame thy heart,
For fresh-cut logs are difficult to burn alone.

---

¹ *Lit.* The oriental imagery of this verse is hard to render. It
might be translated :
  Do not disorder (*or* make curly) thine hyacinthine hair,
  Do not dim with blood-stained tears thy drunken narcissus-eyes.
  Thou art bent on cutting off thy love from me;
  Time will cut it off—do not hasten on.

² *Lit.* "O stony-hearted one, thou pitiest me not."

38.

My heart is giddy and distraught for love of thee,
And tears in torrents flood my beating eyes;[1]
How like a new-cut log are lovers' hearts,
Whilst one end burns, the other bleeds its sap.

39.

Without thee my heart has no moment's peace,
And if I see thy face my grief has fled ;
If all men had a share in my heart's grief,
No heart in all the world but would be sad.

40.

Thy tangled curls are scattered o'er thy face,
Mingling the Roses with the Hyacinths ;
But part asunder those entangled strands,
On every hair thou'lt find there hangs a heart.

41.

O may thy sunny face grow brighter yet,
May thy love's arrow split my heart in twain ;
Knowest thou why thy cheek's mole is so black ?
All things become burnt black close to the sun !

Lit. If I so much as strike my eyelashes together a torrent arises.

42.

The breeze that played amid[1] thy curling locks
Is sweeter far than hyacinths to me ;
All night I pressed thy picture on my breast,[2]
At dawn my bed gave forth a scent of roses.

43.

With two strands of thy hair will I string my
　　rebāb,
In my wretched state what canst thou ask of me ?
Seeing that thou hast no wish to be my Love,
Why comest thou each midnight, in my sleep ?

44.

O thou whose sweet soft eyes the *surmeh* shades,
O thou whose slender figure rends my heart,
O thou whose musky ringlets cluster on thy neck,
Why passest thou unheeding ?—art thou dumb ?

---

[1] *Lit.* comes from the roots (or ' side ') of thy, &c.

[2] *Or,* " All night I clasped thine image (phantom) to my
breast."

45.

Love to be sweet must be reciprocal,
Love unrequited maketh sick the heart;
If Majnūn's heart was desperate for love,
The heart of Leila was more desperate still.

46.

Come and illume my chamber for one night,
Keep me not wretched by thine absence from me;[1]
By the two arcs that are thine eyebrows' curves, I swear
Since thou 'st forgotten, Grief only shares my bed.

47.

Art thou a lion or leopard, O Heart, O Heart,
That thou warrest ever with me, O Heart, O Heart ?
Fall thou into my hands; I'll spill thy blood,
To see what colour it is, O Heart, O Heart !

48.

My Beautiful ! thou hast my heart and soul,
Thou hast mine inner and mine outer self;
I know not why I am so very sad,
I only know that thou hold'st the remedy.

---

[1] *Lit.* Do not leave me in the affliction of the day of separation.

49.

Comest thou thyself?[1] I will cover thee with caresses,
Comest thou not?[2] for thine absence will I sorely
grieve.[3]
Be thy sorrows[4] what they may, lay them upon my
heart,
And I will either die of them, or be consumed by them,
or bear them bravely.

50.

Seven days the anemones last upon the heights,
On river-brink the violets last seven days;
From town to town will I proclaim this truth,
" But seven days can rosy cheeks keep faith ! "

51.

Grieving for thee my heart is ever sad,
A brick my pillow, and my couch the earth ;
My only sin is loving thee too well :
Surely not all thy lovers suffer so ?

---

[1] *Lit.* If thou comest, by thy life I will, &c.
[2] *Lit.* And if thou comest not.
[3] *Lit.* will I melt.
[4] I.e. the pains thou canst inflict.

52.

A taper I, whose flame sheds waxen tears,[1]
Are not the tears from burning hearts the same?
All night I burn, throughout the day I weep,
Such days and nights are all on thine account.

53.

When thou'rt away mine eyes o'erflow with tears,
Barren the Tree of Hope when thou'rt away;
Without thee, night and day, in a solitary corner,
I sit, till life itself come to an end.

54.

O Heart! I mourn in purple for thy flight,
I bear my grief as the train-bearer bears the train;
As the dawn boasts the rising Sun, boast I thy love,
Henceforth till Israfil shall sound his trump.

---

[1] *Lit.* whose tears are of fire. Cf. the verse of Jamāl 'ud-dīn Salmān quoted by Sir Gore Ouseley ("Biographical Notices of Persian Poets," London, 1846) beginning:

شمع خود سوخت شب دوش بزاری

"Last night the taper consumed itself weeping sorrow" (at our separation).

55.

Full is my heart with fire and mine eyes with tears,
Brim full the vessel of my life with grief ;[1]
But dead, I should revive with thy perfume,
If haply thou shouldst wander o'er my grave.

*   *   *   *

56.

Fate is an ill that no one can avert,
It wields its sway alike o'er Kings and Viziers ;
The King who yesterday, by his rule, devoured Kerman,
Becomes to-day himself the meat of worms.[2]

57.

Black is my lot, my fortune 's overturned,[3]
Ruined are my fortunes, for my luck is brought low ;[4]
A thorn, a thistle I, on the Mountain of Love,
For my heart's sake.[5]   Drown it in blood, O Lord !

---

[1] *Lit.* with my heart's blood.
[2] Observe the note to the text on page 59.
[3] *Lit.* topsy-turvy.
[4] *Lit.* overturned.
[5] *Lit.* By my heart's doing.

58.

Since that First Day when Thou createdst us,
What hast Thou seen in us save frowardness?
Lord! by the Faith of Thy blest Twelve Imāms
Forget Thou seest for us the Camel of Death.

59.

The Age's grief is our Soul's portion here,
To free our Souls from care needs magic[1] art;
To all, at last, comes remedy for grief,
Annihilation cures all hearts at last.[2]

60.

I go, I depart, I leave this world of ours,
I journey beyond the furthest bounds of Chīn,[3]
And, journeying, ask Pilgrims about the Road,
"Is this the End?[4] or must I journey on?"

---

[1] *Lit.* alchemy.
[2] *Lit.* It is (only) our heart whose (sole) remedy is annihilation.
[3] چین و ماچین is supposed to mean "China and Manchuria."
[4] *Lit.* Is this distance enough?

61.

My new-born Vision of Beauty, where art thou?
Where art thou with thy *surmeh*-shaded eyes?
The Soul of Ṭāhir struggles to be free,
And, at this Supreme Moment, where art thou?[1]

*   *   *   *

62.

O man who ne'er hast studied Heavenly Lore,
Nor set thy foot within the Tavern-doors,
Thou knowest not what thou hast escaped or gained;
How shalt thou come among the Elect? Alas!

---

[1] *Lit.* Breath (of Life) has come to Ṭāhir's bosom.
  Just as it is time to depart (die): Where art thou, O
  my dear one?

TEACHINGS OF RUMI: THE MASNAVI

The greatest mystical poet of any age

Professor R. A. Nicolson

It can well be argued that he is the supreme mystical poet of all mankind

Professor A. J. Arberry

The Masnavi is full of profound mysteries, and a most important book in the study of Sufism – mysteries which must, for the most part, be left to the discernment of the reader

F. Hadland Davis

Rumi was not only a poet and a mystic and the founder of a religious order; he was also a man of profound insight into the nature of man

Professor Erich Fromm

To the Sufi, if not to anyone else, this book speaks from a different dimension, yet a dimension which is in a way within his deepest self

Idries Shah

The depth and beauty of its thoughts find fitting expression in the language in which they are conveyed, which is composed with consummate skill

Professor C. E. Wilson

He makes plain to the Pilgrim the secrets of the Way of Unity, and unveils the Mysteries of the Path of Eternal Truth

Dr. Samuel Johnson

TEACHINGS OF RUMI: THE MASNAVI
Abridged & Translated by E. H. Whinfield
With an Introduction by Idries Shah
The Octagon Press

SADI:
THE ROSE GARDEN

Sadi's *Gulistan, The Rose Garden*, is both one of the best-known of the Sufi classics and a major work of Persian literature.

Sheikh Sadi (circa 1184 – circa 1292) of Shiraz, studied in Baghdad and travelled widely in India, Africa and the Arab world. He was a pupil of the eminent Sufi Sheikh Shahabuddin Suhrawardi, and his works have been translated into many Western languages.

'These are not essays or disquisitions; each is a little landscape of tales, maxims, aphorisms, reminiscences, verse and poetry in different manners . . . singularly attractive'

Books and Bookmen

SADI: THE ROSE GARDEN
Translated by Edward B. Eastwick CB, MA, FRS, MRAS
With an Introduction by Idries Shah
The Octagon Press

A PERFUMED SCORPION

The 'perfuming of a scorpion' referred to by the great Sufi teacher Bahaudin symbolises hypocrisy and self-deception: both in the individual and in institutions.

Idries Shah, in these lectures and meditations, directs attention to both the perfume and the scorpion – the overlay and the reality – in psychology, human behaviour and the learning process.

Crammed with illustrative anecdotes from contemporary life, the book is nevertheless rooted in the teaching patterns of Rumi, Hafiz, Jami and many other great sages. It deals with the need for, and ways to, knowledge as well as information, understanding which comes beyond belief, perception as distinct from emotion, self-development in addition to the desire for intellectuality.

'Suppose Einstein had "leaked" one aspect of his Relativity concept to an astronomer, another aspect to, say, a biologist and so on. It seems likely that small revolutions would quickly have followed in different branches of science without anybody suspecting the existence of a master. Something like this may be happening today.... Idries Shah, the 53-year-old Afghan appears to be the man-behind-the-scenes in all this . . .'

Evening News

A PERFUMED SCORPION
by Idries Shah
The Octagon Press

TEACHINGS OF HAFIZ

Hafiz of Shiraz is unquestionably in the front rank of world classical poets. As a lyricist and Sufi master, his work is celebrated from India to Central Asia and the Near East as are Shakespeare, Dante or Milton in the West: Goethe himself, among many other Westerners, was among the Master's admirers.

As Professor Shafaq says:

'Hafiz attained perfect mystical consciousness: and his spiritual and mental power derived from this. The Path, projected by Sana'i, Attar, Rumi and Sa'di each in his own way, is described by Hafiz with the very deepest feeling and highest expressive achievement. His lyrics encapsulate the materials treated by others only at great length. So deeply immersed is he in mystical unity that, no matter the formal subject of his writing, every ode and lyric contains evidence of this sublime theme.'

History of Persian Literature, Tehran

This collection is by the eminent linguist and explorer Gertrude Bell who (as Dr. A. J. Arberry says) 'early in her adventurous life conceived an enthusiasm for Hafiz which compelled her to write a volume of very fine translations'.

TEACHINGS OF HAFIZ
Collected & Translated by Gertrude Bell
With an Introduction by Idries Shah
The Octagon Press